Original title:

Peach Blossoms and Daydreams

Copyright © 2025 Creative Arts Management OÜ
All rights reserved.

Author: Julian Prescott
ISBN HARDBACK: 978-1-80586-348-9
ISBN PAPERBACK: 978-1-80586-820-0

The Heartbeat of Blossoming Thoughts

In a tangle of petals, I find my stride,
With bees that buzz, my thoughts collide.
A sneeze erupts, oh, what a show,
The gardening gnome laughs, 'twas quite the blow!

With every bloom, a chuckle grows,
The squirrels dance, striking silly poses.
The sun gives a wink, the sky dimples bright,
While rabbits plot mischief, ready for flight.

Daylight Drifts through Floral Lanes

As light spills laughter on grassy knolls,
A butterfly winks and juggles whole rolls.
With petals like feathers around us flit,
Even the ants tap dance, what a wild skit!

In the midst of blooms, a cat takes a snooze,
While overzealous frogs croak out their blues.
The sky mumbles secrets in soft, silly tones,
While roses gossip in fancy flower thrones.

Cascades of Colorful Reverie

Colors burst forth like a joyous stampede,
A parade of daisies, not one but a breed.
With giggles of tulips and laughter of stems,
The garden grows livelier than all of our friends.

But wait! Here's a snail, in its 'racing' disguise,
Taking its time with awesome surprise.
The foxglove snickers, the lilacs rejoice,
In this whimsical patch, we all have a voice!

A Garden of Gracious Thought

Imagine a space where ideas clash,
With daisies quipping a funny little mash.
The raindrops write poems, adorning the leaves,
While wisps of old thoughts hang on, like thieves.

A wise old tortoise attempts to explain,
'Slow down, dear friends, through madness comes gain!'
With snickers and snorts in a wacky run,
A garden of giggles, where thoughts weigh a ton.

Petal Kisses on a Cloudy Day

Soft petals twirl and sway,
A bee gets lost, oh what a play!
He thinks he's found a hidden snack,
But finds a spider ready to attack.

Rain clouds loom, but laughter flies,
With flying hats and silly pies.
A gust of wind, a funny chase,
We trip and roll in nature's grace.

Underneath the Canopy of Wonder.

Beneath the leaves where squirrels scamper,
A rabbit sneezes, what a pamper!
The flowers giggle, swaying to greet,
As bugs start dancing on tiny feet.

A picnic spread, oh what delight,
Sandwiches hop, taking flight!
With lemonade that squirts a stream,
Every sip turns into a dream.

Whispers of Spring's Embrace

The breeze whispers jokes, oh so sly,
A butterfly sneezes, oh my, oh my!
The daffodils hide, pulling away,
While tulips chuckle in bright display.

In a field where daisies roam,
A bumblebee tries finding home.
But gets lost in a circus feat,
Balancing pollen on tiny feet.

A Dance Beneath the Petals

In a swirl of colors, blooms take the floor,
A dancing flower can't take it anymore!
With a spin and a twirl, they sway with glee,
As the ants join in, what a sight to see!

A ladybug leads, in her polka-dot dress,
While grasshoppers leap, oh what a mess!
They stumble and giggle, on this grand stage,
A funny ballet at their merry age.

Dreams Adrift on Gentle Breezes

On fluffy clouds, I start to float,
With giggles in each silly note.
A kite on strings, I'm pulled along,
Chasing whispers, skipping songs.

Lemonade spills on my new dress,
I twirl and laugh, I must confess.
A trampoline made of candy canes,
I bounce my way through friendly rains.

Petal-Kissed Memories

A memory pops like a bubble gum,
I chew on laughter, can't be glum.
Butterflies dance in silly pairs,
Twirling like they forgot their cares.

Sticky fingers on chocolate bars,
I'm running wild, I'm reaching stars.
With sunshine painted on my face,
I find my joy in the fastest place.

In the Garden of Fleeting Thoughts

In a garden where giggles grow,
I chase the thoughts that twist and flow.
A rabbit wears a floppy hat,
He tells me tales of a dancing cat.

Grinning flowers wink at me,
They share the secrets of a bumblebee.
Together we splash in puddles wide,
Silly surprises we cannot hide.

The Color of Hope

A rainbow sprinkles in the sky,
I hop beneath, I want to fly.
Each color shouts a quirky rhyme,
Telling jokes about lost time.

With crayons bright, I draw my dreams,
Ice cream rivers, wobbly streams.
I dance in fields of marshmallow fluff,
With laughter oozing, that's enough!

Sun-Kissed Mornings and Petal Secrets

In the garden where laughter plays,
Sunshine dances in a lazy haze.
Squirrels play tag in the morning mist,
While bees prance in a floral tryst.

The daisies giggle, a secret crew,
Making fun of the roses too.
A butterfly lands on a clownish rose,
Pretending to check if it's ticklish, who knows?

With each bloom, a story unfolds,
Of witty whispers only nature holds.
They tease the clouds, fluffy and grand,
Hoping to trip them, just for a hand!

The Scent of Idle Whispers

A breeze hums tunes from afar,
Tickling petals, like a merry bazaar.
Lemons laugh in the sunny shell,
Citrusy jokes they tell so well.

Underneath a feeble tree,
An ant questions life's mystery.
Why do birds always sing so loud?
Are they just trying to annoy the crowd?

The tulips gossip, oh what a show,
They mimic the wind with a dramatic flow.
And the daffodils rolling in delight,
Chasing shadows till the fall of night.

Petals Unfurling in Solitude

In the quiet of a playful breeze,
Petals stretch out, doing as they please.
A lone flower yawns at the dawn,
Wondering why all the fun is gone.

A snail rolls by with a dreamy sigh,
Trying to catch raindrops falling shy.
He grumbles about the slow parade,
While dancing dew drops steal the shade.

Nearby, a tulip tells a joke,
About a bee that couldn't poke.
The petals giggle, turn bright red,
Wishing for laughter instead of dread.

Dappled Dreams of the Orchard

In the orchard where shadows play,
Fruits make faces, come what may.
Cherries debate if they're round or square,
While apples chuckle, like they don't care.

A rambunctious breeze steals more than a glance,
Upsetting the pears in a fanciful dance.
They blush and rustle, trying to flee,
From the giggling shadows beneath the tree.

The squirrels, they tap on the trunk so low,
Challenging branches to join the show.
Mirth in the air, with laughter so loud,
Even the clouds cannot help but be proud.

Fragrant Dreams Unfurled

In a garden where giggles play,
Petals twirl like dancers in ballet.
Bees wear tiny hats, quite the sight,
Buzzing jokes from morning till night.

Sunshine spills its golden cheer,
While squirrels practice their mime careers.
The flowers laugh, a fragrant scent,
Wishing for a party they never rent.

A ladybug trips, spreads her arms wide,
And falls on a leaf with a whimsical glide.
The breeze whispers secrets in a soft tone,
While trees giggle under the blue dome.

Rain clouds play hide and seek with the sun,
Puffing up, then bursting for fun.
Each droplet a laugh, splashing on grass,
Nature's comedy, in a sunny class.

A Serenade to Morning's Charm

Early birds wear pajamas, it's true,
Chirping tunes as they sip morning dew.
Worms dance a jig, all wriggly and spry,
Under a sky that's a pancake pie.

The sun yawns wide, its golden frown,
Tickling clouds with a sleepy brown.
While flowers attempt to comb their hair,
And bees declare it a pollen affair.

A butterfly winks with one painted eye,
While ants march on, trying to fly.
With fame and glitter, they plan their show,
But keep tripping over the roots below.

Laughter rings out, it's a musical day,
Nature conducts in its quirky way.
Every petal a laugh, every breeze a grin,
Join the morning's dance, let the fun begin!

Fluttering Hopes in a Petal Sea

In a field where whimsy takes flight,
Butterflies roast marshmallows at night.
The moon cracks jokes, full of delight,
While crickets chirp their laughs, oh so bright.

A daisy paints stars in a sky so high,
While ladybugs gossip, oh my, oh my!
Each petal a canvas for their great dreams,
Sprinkling laughter like sunbeams and creams.

Grasshoppers strut with an air of flair,
Donning funny shoes, without a care.
The wind steals hats from the flowers' heads,
As blossoms chuckle in their cozy beds.

A sunflower poses, strikes a bold stance,
While tulips tiptoe, joining the dance.
Fluttering hopes in a colorful spree,
Life's too funny, let's giggle with glee!

Echoing Lullabies in Soft Fields

Under the shade, I took a nap,
A squirrel stole my sandwich, oh what a trap!
Butterflies danced, wearing polka dots,
While I chased my dreams in forget-me-nots.

The wind giggled, like an old friend,
Telling secrets that would never end.
I slipped on grass, a comedic sight,
And laughed at my fall beneath the sunlight.

Clouds above played a game of tag,
While ants marched on with a tiny flag.
Jokes from the daisies, sweet and spry,
Whispering funny tales as they waved goodbye.

In a soft field where laughter sings,
Nature's humor has the lightest wings.
With each breeze, a chuckle takes flight,
Leaving me wondering, is this all right?

A Voyage Through Fragrant Haze

In the garden of scents, I took a tour,
With lilies gossiping, always wanting more.
Roses snickered at the daffodils,
While aromas swirled like whimsical quills.

Through the haze where laughter blooms,
The bees collect jokes, buzz with grooms.
I lost my hat to a playful breeze,
As flowers chuckled, swaying with ease.

Caterpillars in tiny top hats twirled,
While ladybugs plotted mischief, unfurled.
With each step, I slipped on petals bright,
And giggled at my unexpected flight.

This fragrant voyage, so silly and sweet,
Turned my daydreams into a comic treat.
In a world of laughter, nothing's amiss,
With every bloom comes a crazy bliss.

Alchemy of Color and Bliss

With a splash of hues, I dipped my brush,
Creating a rainbow in a wild rush.
The colors giggled, jumbled in play,
As each brush stroke whispered, "Let's sway!"

Frogs in top hats croaked their delight,
While splatters of pink gave a marvelous fright.
Each canvas a jester, laughing aloud,
Winks from zephyrs, taking a bow.

The sky unleashed its colors divine,
As I danced 'round puddles, feeling just fine.
Clumsy and silly, I twirled with flair,
As shades of madness floated in air.

This alchemy spins joy into art,
Transforming my frown into laughter's heart.
In colors so vibrant, I find my sound,
Where happiness blooms, and silliness abound.

The Enchantment of a Quiet Afternoon

In stillness, the shadows have a chat,
While time sips tea, like a witty cat.
A chair with wheels rolled away in glee,
As sunlight giggled, saying, "Catch me!"

The clock tickled my nose with a tease,
While I leaned back, trying to appease.
With a yawn and a stretch, the day grew bright,
Mysteries danced in the fading light.

Birds sang ballads that made no sense,
As squirrels played chess; quite an expense!
Each soft sigh of wind brought giggles anew,
Whispering secrets only the trees knew.

In this magic hour, silliness reigns,
Bringing joy through the soft, gentle rains.
With laughter echoing through each embrace,
An afternoon's charm left a smile on my face.

Embrace of Blossom and Sky

Amidst the chatter of buzzing bees,
A squirrel steals my sandwich with ease.
Laughter erupts like petals in spring,
As I ponder the joy that such chaos can bring.

Floating clouds giggle and dance with delight,
While I chase butterflies, losing my sight.
A daisy plays peek-a-boo, oh what a scene,
In a world where nothing is ever too mean.

Drifting in a Fragrant Mirage

Fragrant whispers tickle my nose,
As goofy raccoons put on a show.
They juggle acorns and dance on a log,
While I sip lemonade, feeling like a fog.

Funky mushrooms sway in bright colors,
Inviting me to party with other mothers.
We twirl through fields, so carefree and loud,
As daisies laugh, saying we're quite the crowd.

Beneath the Blushing Boughs

Underneath the branches so spry,
A bouncy rabbit makes me sigh.
With floppy ears and wiggly toes,
He's my comedic muse in splendid repose.

As shadows dance and tickle the ground,
I find funny faces in blooms all around.
The flowers giggle, whispering chic,
With every breeze, they pull a quick trick.

Sweet Delirium under Azure

The sky wraps us in a playful hug,
While I search for worms, but find only a slug.
Yet laughter bubbles like a fizzy drink,
As I join a parade led by a sprightly pink.

Bubbles float, carrying wishes galore,
As playful clouds knock on imagination's door.
With every pop, the jokes come alive,
In a world where silliness is sure to thrive.

Where Horizons Meet Petals

Beneath the trees with hats of pink,
A bumblebee, it starts to drink.
With giggles floating through the air,
We watch the clouds and lose our care.

The grass beneath is ticklish soft,
While butterflies do silly lofts.
A dance-off starts with clumsy feet,
Who knew this place would be so sweet?

The breeze joins in with tricks to tease,
Each flower bows as if to please.
We laugh until the sun goes down,
Our silly jokes, our comic crown.

So here we sit with tea so bright,
In petals' shade, it feels just right.
Let's keep this laughter close and near,
For moments like these bring us cheer.

Melodies of the Ever-Changing Sky

The clouds above, a cotton toll,
Claiming dreams like a donut roll.
A sunbeam sprinkles joy on kids,
While squirrels steal snacks, oh those sneaky bids!

We chase the shadows, weave our tales,
With jokes so funny, like fish with scales.
As raindrops tap a playful tune,
We share our quirks, a silly boon.

The stars at night, they wink and nod,
As if to say, 'You're a bit odd!'
We dance with crickets, sing with frogs,
Beneath the glow of sleepy logs.

In this wild garden where laughter grows,
Imagination's path freely flows.
Each twist and turn brings playful glee,
So let's create our own jamboree!

A Symphony of Color and Light

A canvas bright with mishaps clear,
A dandelion called, "I'm over here!"
As paint drips down from clumsy hands,
We giggle loud, ignoring plans.

The palette spills like laughter light,
Mixing blues of day and stars of night.
Each stroke a shout, a silly dance,
A masterpiece made by pure chance.

So here we twirl through shades so wacky,
A rainbow cake, our moments tacky.
With colors bright, our smiles grow,
Chunky handprints in a funny show.

As daylight fades, the colors blend,
We smile at all this art we send.
Life's a canvas, come take a seat,
Let's paint together; oh, what a feat!

Threads of Serene Moments

In cozy corners, laughter weaves,
With silly tales, like bumblebees.
We knit our dreams with threads of fun,
Each stitch a whim, and then we run.

A cozy chair, a blanket tight,
Imagination takes us high as flight.
With quirky thoughts that bounce around,
In this warm nest, pure joy is found.

A teapot spills absurdity bright,
While shadows dance in soft twilight.
We share our hopes and giggles sweet,
A tapestry of joy complete.

So gather 'round this happy space,
Let laughter line each woven trace.
With every giggle, it's clear to see,
These threads will bind our memory.

Chasing Cloud-Kissed Fantasies

In a garden full of giggles,
A rabbit stole my sandwich,
I chased him through the tickling grass,
He laughed, 'Catch me if you can!'

Butterflies wore tiny glasses,
Debating on the best flower,
While daisies danced in fine tuxedos,
Competing for sun's brightest hour.

A hedgehog tried to juggle snacks,
But tripped and rolled in confetti,
We all just burst into laughter,
As the sun felt light and petty.

So let's prance in silly circles,
With whimsy dressing up our minds,
In this land of cloud-kissed laughter,
Where reality is hard to find.

Blooms and the Art of Daylight

Under the sun's bright canvas,
A bumblebee wore a bow tie,
He danced with flowers, oh so clumsy,
Making all the garden sigh.

The tulips giggled in a row,
Telling tales of shy old trees,
While daisies tried to tell a joke,
But forgot it with the breeze.

A squirrel hung from the swing,
His acorns stacked like vintage chairs,
He juggled them while proudly singing,
A tune from years of forest fairs.

So join this merry revelry,
Underneath the sky's bright art,
Where every bloom and sunny ray,
Tickles gently at the heart.

Reveries on a Breezy Afternoon

Fluffy clouds in a playful race,
Chasing after chairs of wind,
Where children laugh and run in place,
While plans for snacks are whimsically pinned.

An ant in shades dashes along,
With tiny tunes playing on repeat,
While puffy seeds join in the throng,
Twisting and twirling on their feet.

The sun peeked through, a cheeky grin,
With butterflies as its boisterous crew,
They tossed confetti of pollen and skin,
As laughter lingered like morning dew.

So let's flutter beneath warm rays,
In this dream of colors and sounds,
Where whimsy sprinkles sunny plays,
And joy in every moment abounds.

A Tapestry of Floral Dreams

A seamstress weaves with threads of light,
Stitching laughs between each bloom,
While daisies flip their petals bright,
Broadening smiles, sewing out gloom.

The wind sings songs of chases past,
With giggles wrapped in cotton candy,
As bees perform their dizzy dance,
Clumsy yet oh-so-handy!

While ladybugs plot their next great scheme,
To host a party on a leaf,
All while the sun grins in a beam,
Turning each moment into a brief.

So skip through fields of vibrant cheer,
In this tapestry, laughter's theme,
Where every petal holds a beer,
And life unfolds like one funny dream.

Of Luscious Hues and Soft Silhouettes

In gardens where laughter grows,
Colors burst in funny shows,
A squirrel in a top hat prances,
While a gopher tries to take his chances.

Breezes tickle the cherry trees,
As bumblebees dance with ease,
Two ants argue over crumbs of cake,
While a butterfly hops like a cheerful quake.

All around, the sky's a hue,
And clouds poke fun; they're quite askew,
A few petals drift, they throw a fit,
Saying, 'Why not land, here's where you sit.'

So let's giggle at nature's crew,
In this realm where joy breaks through,
Amidst the hues, our hearts align,
In laughter's embrace, everything's fine.

The Allure of Chasing Shadows

Shadows skip across the ground,
In a game where laughter's found,
Chasing each other, they trip and fall,
While we all cheer, 'Come on, give it your all!'

A cat joins in, with grace so sly,
Its shadow leaps, oh my, oh my!
In a whirl of giggles, we lose track,
As shadows lead us along their track.

Each step a riddle, each pause a tease,
As the sun dips low, they dance with ease,
Their playful prance, a sight to behold,
A tale of folly, both bright and bold.

So here we stand, all laughter and cheer,
Finding joy in what's unclear,
Where shadows play, and spirits rise,
In the chaos of dusk, our laughter flies.

Patterns of Light in Petal Pools

In a pool of petals, colors blend,
A catfish swims, just around the bend,
With sunglasses on, it winks all day,
While pigeons argue over who gets to play.

Lemonade stands with quirky signs,
While bees sip nectar, sipping their wines,
And weeds wear hats made of old tin cans,
As the trees hum tunes, with claps from their fans.

Sunshine dances with a playful kick,
As clouds throw water balloons—they're slick!
With every splash, laughter erupts,
In a garden where giggles forever disrupt.

So let's dive in, laughter awaits,
Amidst the petals, let's celebrate,
From pollen parties to sunbeam cheers,
In this whimsical realm, shed all your fears.

Tales Woven with Vivid Threads

A loom spins yarns of silly fights,
Where sparrows stitch capes for kite flights,
And kittens embroider with strings of gold,
We weave our tales, both brave and bold.

Grasshopper's jokes make daisies sway,
Telling puns that brighten the day,
In a patchwork of giggles, we spin around,
Where laughter's the fabric, so snug and sound.

Every color tells a story so grand,
As the wind tickles petals across the land,
We stitch our dreams in every hue,
Creating a quilt of joy, just for you.

So gather round, let's share some glee,
In this tapestry, forever free,
With threads of laughter, we joyfully tread,
In a world where silliness is widely spread.

The Palette of Drowsy Dreams

In a world where clouds taste sweet,
Colors drip from lazy feet,
Pineapples dance on rainbow beams,
While kittens plot their silly schemes.

A yellow hat floats by my head,
It whispers dreams of sleepy bread,
A polka-dotted chair sings loud,
Inviting me to join the crowd.

Jellybeans grow on every tree,
Bouncing loudly, oh so free,
A giggle tickles my bright shoe,
As ants parade in wacky hue.

So come and join this weary fight,
Where shadows play in soft moonlight,
And laughter echoes through the air,
With gummy bears and jelly flair.

Serendipity in Full Bloom

A llama danced in polka dots,
Too busy dreaming, tying knots,
He juggles pies and lots of cake,
With every move, the world will shake.

Sunflowers wear the strangest hats,
While squirrels chirp like crazy bats,
They hold a party in the breeze,
Where everyone just wants to tease.

A rainbow slides down from the sky,
It tumbles, giggles, oh so spry,
With fountains filled with fizzy cheer,
And all our worries disappear.

So take a seat on clouds of fluff,
With candy shoes and furry stuff,
Let's paint our giggles on the ground,
In vibrant colors, fun unbound.

Carried by the Winds of Imagination

A paper plane flies high and free,
It whispers tales of you and me,
With every turn, it tells a joke,
While jumping beans begin to smoke.

A wiggly worm dons fairy wings,
Reciting silly songs it sings,
With cupcakes swaying in the breeze,
And dancing leaves upon the trees.

Balloons that giggle in the sky,
Invite the butterflies to fly,
Together, laughter paints the day,
In swirls of colors, bright and gay.

So hop along this whimsical ride,
Where magic sparks and dreams abide,
With every breath, let chuckles bloom,
And lift our hearts from any gloom.

Echoes of Soft Laughter

In a meadow full of whimsy sounds,
The daisies dance on playful grounds,
A fuzzy bee makes silly trails,
While turtles tell the best of tales.

The sun wears shades and spins around,
Chasing shadows that won't be found,
With giggles bouncing on the streams,
As ducks join in with wobbly dreams.

A squirrel rides a pogo stick,
Squeaking out a perfect trick,
While clouds begin a tickle fight,
As laughter sparkles in the light.

So skip along and play your tune,
With pies that giggle at the moon,
For every chuckle spreads the cheer,
In echoing whispers, soft and clear.

Hues of a Delicate Day

In a garden where giggles grow,
A cat in a hat steals the show.
Bunnies hop in mismatched shoes,
Chasing butterflies with silly views.

The sun winks with a golden cheer,
While ants parade without a fear.
A squirrel juggles acorns in flight,
As frogs croak jokes, it's pure delight.

The flowers laugh, their colors bright,
As pixies dance on beams of light.
Each blade of grass sings a tune,
Frolicking 'neath a cheeky moon.

What fun to frolic, jump, and play,
In this whimsical, silly day!
Let giggles echo, let's have a blast,
In this haven where joy will last.

Harvest of Tranquility

Beneath the tree where shadows sway,
A bear in shades enjoys the day.
Birds critique his lazy pose,
Seagulls snicker at his toes.

Kites flutter above with glee,
While ants bring snacks for their tea.
The breeze brings whispers, tales so grand,
Of the squirrel's last birthday band.

With laughter rippling all around,
Where giggles bloom from the ground.
A picnic blanket curls with smiles,
As friends all gather in funny styles.

And when the light begins to fade,
They plan the fun that will cascade.
For every giggle and soft sigh,
Is a treasure that will never die.

Cascades of Whispered Wishes

In a meadow of dreams and fluff,
A duck quacks riddles, oh so tough.
The clouds snicker as kites take flight,
Painting patterns of pure delight.

Each daisy winks with a secret grin,
As lions roll on their chins.
The wind carries tales of silly fights,
Where crickets compose symphonies at nights.

A snail in a race, slow and grand,
Mocks the hare who can't understand.
Puddles reflect smiles, bright and bold,
In this crazy world, joy unfolds.

With whimsical breezes, laughter flows,
Tickling noses with sweet repose.
May wishes gather like fluffy clouds,
In a life where laughter loudly crowds.

Drifting on Petal-Laden Dreams

On a river of petals, we sail away,
With giggles and guffaws that brighten the day.
A turtle dons a sailor's hat,
While frogs critique his fashion pat.

The sun sets low, a cheeky light,
With fireflies glowing in playful flight.
Each ripple reflects a shimmered grin,
As silly whispers dance in the wind.

The owls hoot in duet so rare,
Telling tall tales without a care.
With dreams like balloons, we drift on by,
Under a starlit, gleeful sky.

In this carnival of carefree streams,
We float away on laughter beams.
For in this realm, we find our muse,
In smiling moments we can't refuse.

Starlit Promises Beneath Tender Canopies

Under the moon's playful wink,
The trees whisper secrets in pink,
I made a pact with the breeze,
To tickle my toes and tease.

A squirrel donned a tiny hat,
Claiming he's quite the diplomat,
He'll negotiate with the stars,
For cakes and cookies from Mars!

Fireflies join in a dance,
With twinkling lights, they prance,
The flowers giggle in delight,
As night turns the world light!

Waking up from such mischief,
I wonder if dreams were too stiff,
Maybe my pact was too bold,
Next time, I'll stick to tales told.

The Language of Floating Petals

Petals float like whispers soft,
In gardens where giggles are oft,
A bee dons shades, buzzing around,
'Is it sunny, or am I just wound?'

A snail with swagger takes the lead,
In this wacky race to succeed,
He shouts, 'I'm faster than you think!'
While drifting in a marzipan ink!

Butterflies with tales so grand,
Tell of cookies from a far-off land,
Where laughter grows on every tree,
And every snack is wild and free!

With petals as letters they send,
To squirrels, their mischievous friends,
Banter floats on the breeze's whim,
In a world so abundantly grim!

A Portrait of Sweet Daydreams

A painter splashed the sky with fun,
While donuts and laughter spun,
Smoky clouds made candy shapes,
As ice cream trucks played funny tapes!

A hapless cat in a tailor's suit,
Swings from a swing made of fruit,
'Life is good when you add a slice,'
He purred, 'Especially if it's nice!'

Wishing wells filled with goldfish dreams,
Sing songs of chocolate and moonbeams,
Giggles mix with the pitter-patter,
As time flies, who cares? It's all chatter!

The night closes with a grand parade,
Of cookies and cupcakes, nicely laid,
In this painting of sweet delight,
Life's a canvas, painted right!

Swaying in the Woven Breeze

The wind spins tales so absurd,
As laughter dances like a bird,
A group of leaves, sharing a jest,
'Who wore the fanciest vest?'

The flowers giggle and twirl in glee,
Some think they're just too free,
They crown the ants at their tiny ball,
Holding court, 'You're the best of all!'

A dandelion winks with flair,
Claiming it knows how to scare,
But all that comes out is a puff,
Leaving the wind to say, 'That's enough!'

In all this wriggle and wiggle,
Life's too fun to just be a giggle,
So we sway in this woven air,
Finding joy in laughter, everywhere!

Sunlit Reverie

In the sun, I sip my tea,
A butterfly flies right at me.
I think it's there to steal my drink,
Or is it just a flirty wink?

A bird sings songs of pure delight,
While squirrels plot their next big fight.
The daisies giggle, tickled by breeze,
And I'm just sitting here, at ease.

My hat's all crooked on my head,
I wish I'd rather stayed in bed.
But laughter bubbles in the air,
While I toss crumbs to a fluffy bear.

The clouds parade in silly hats,
And I can't help but chat with cats.
They laugh aloud at my display,
As I twirl in my own array.

The Scent of Soft Delights

The breeze carries scents of sweet cheer,
Honey and giggles draw all near.
I trip on grass—oh, what a sight!
A tumble brings them sheer delight.

The little frogs in wild ballet,
Jump and croak in their goofy way.
They wave their tiny legs and cheer,
As I dance while drinking my beer.

A ladybug spots me on the ground,
Winks and whispers, 'You're quite profound!'
I'm left giggling, what a life!
I'm just a star, they're all my wife!

I chase my dreams, much like a pup,
And trip over a paint-filled cup.
But splashy colors brighten my mood,
As I laugh with nature, oh so rude!

Beneath the Canopy of Wishes

Under leaves, I toss a coin,
Wishing for a snack, not disappointment.
The wind just giggles, plays its tricks,
And sends me bouncing on some sticks.

The shadows dance like playful sprites,
Twirling around, igniting delights.
Each step I take, a squeaky squeal,
As I fool around like a silly eel.

A flower pops up, saying, 'Hello!'
And I reply, 'You're quite the show!'
Together we craft a funny scene,
With laughter blooming where we've been.

So let's rejoice in this sunny patch,
With quirky creatures and a funny match.
For life's a jest beneath this dome,
Where every breath feels just like home!

A Tangle of Sweetness and Shade

In the shade, I find a gnome,
With patchwork pants and no real home.
He chuckles softly, shares his pie,
'You're welcome here, but don't be shy!'

A tickle fight with butterflies,
Who flutter past with silly cries.
They pull my hair like cheeky friends,
In this sweet chaos, joy transcends.

The shadows stretch like playful cats,
While I find jokes in pitter-pats.
Each step I take on leafy trails,
Unveils a world where humor prevails.

So let's sit here and invent our play,
With a gnome, a pie, and a bright bouquet.
In this tangled realm, we're free to roam,
Laughing and dancing, we'll make it home.

Floating on Aromatic Clouds

On a fluffy cloud I lay,
Sipping dreams that drift away.
Butterflies wear silly hats,
And giggle with the chatty cats.

Sunbeams tickle my big toes,
As I float where the laughter grows.
Clouds do the cha-cha in the air,
While rainbows dance without a care.

The breeze pulls pranks on shiny kites,
As everyone enjoys the heights.
If clouds could laugh, they'd laugh out loud,
For silliness is where they're proud.

So I lounge amidst the sky's delight,
Wishing for this day to last all night.
With giggles trailing from the ground,
It's a parade of joy I've found.

When Time Pauses for Wonder

Winding paths of giggle streams,
Where every flower's grown from dreams.
Tick-tock laughs in clockwork trees,
Time stumbles over roots with ease.

Popping bubbles tease the sun,
As silly stories come to run.
Each moment's spun with whimsy's thread,
A tickle fight, it's what I said!

With frolics through the grassy knoll,
The world spins round, but I feel whole.
What's the hurry? Let's just sway,
In wild raptures, come what may.

Time takes a nap, we chase the breeze,
Trapping joy in flowered ease.
When wonder wraps its arms so tight,
We dance, we laugh, till late at night.

Radiance in the Afternoon Glow

Sunshine spills like juice on grass,
Tickling noses as we pass.
Jellybeans call from hidden nooks,
While clouds twist stories in their books.

Playful critters wear bright neon,
As sunlight gleams on their crayon.
It's a carnival of light and sound,
Where mischief makes the world go round.

Lemonade rivers, oh so sweet,
As laughter and smiles chase my feet.
Birds compose a silly song,
Echoing where all is wrong!

With rays that dance like flapping wings,
The day unfolds like a game of kings.
Glow all around fuels my cheer,
In this warm moment, I have no fear.

Laughter Wrapped in Floral Layers

A swirl of petals on my nose,
Silly giggles, where humor grows.
A daisied hat spun from the ground,
In this garden, joy is found.

Bumblebees wear stripy pants,
As I join in their merry dance.
Buttercup tiaras gleam with glee,
Life's a party, come join me!

Ticklish vines curl, wrap me tight,
"Surprise!" they say, a funny sight.
Oh, blooming laughs bloom everywhere,
As joy flutters in fragrant air.

So gather 'round this vibrant space,
Where all the flowers wear a face.
Wrapped in laughter's gentle throng,
We sing our cheerful, silly song.

Sweet Dreams Nestled in Bloom

In a patch of pink, bees start to dance,
They trip over petals, oh what a chance!
A squirrel tells tales of his grand, wild chase,
While we laugh at the clouds that are swirling in lace.

The breeze is a tickler, a gentle tease,
As giggles escape from the rustling leaves.
Kittens nap deeply, dreaming of yarn,
While turtles plot races, but they just yawn.

A rabbit in pajamas hops right on by,
Wearing funky sunglasses and asking us why.
Old birds in a choir sing notes all askew,
And the flowers just giggle, saying, "That's nothing new!"

With cookies for clouds and cakes made of air,
We chew on the giggles we smell everywhere.
In a dreamland of color, we frolic free,
Wrapped in the sweetness of silliness, whee!

Flickers of Light in Flora's Glow

Frogs in top hats croak tunes from the pond,
While fireflies whirl, lighting up a grand bond.
A daisy wore pants that were two sizes too small,
And the roses all giggled, "Look at our pal!"

A dandelion puff tries to act all aloof,
While a butterfly shouts, "Hey, let's have a proof!"
They challenge the wind to a dance-off tonight,
But all they can do is spin left and then right.

With chicken suit clovers, our laughter will swell,
As shadows take turns at a comical spell.
A hedgehog recites poetry in a slow dream,
But ends up just snoring, it's not what it seems!

Yet, through all the giggles, whispers float high,
With each little chuckle, we reach for the sky.
In the glow of the twilight, the fun won't subside,
Flora's bright flickers will brightly abide!

Essence of Spring Lullabies

In a world wrapped in twirls of fragrant delight,
The grass hums a melody, soft as the night.
A hedgehog in slippers lends ears to a tale,
While gophers hold quarrels on who gets the snail.

The clouds wear bright hats and giggle with glee,
As a rooster arrives with a trumpet of 'me!'
He joins in a chorus with bees buzzing cheer,
And all of the blooms laugh, "We'll cheer louder here!"

With petals like confetti, we dance through the day,
Our worries disbanding, just floating away.
A snail with a suitcase is ready to roam,
But a frog on a lily says, "Nah, stay at home!"

Underneath the big moon, all friendships remind,
That laughter and joy in this garden we find.
Wrapped in soft echoes, the night hums along,
In a lullaby language, sweet, silly, and strong.

Vignettes in a Floral Wonderland

In a stretch of pink fields, where odd things take flight,
Turtles on scooters zoom left and right.
A snail on a skateboard races the breeze,
While the daisies debate on the most flowery sneeze.

With each little bloom, stories ripple and swell,
A gopher in glasses knows all quite too well.
"Did you hear what the fern said to the oak?"
But the oak just chuckled, "Oh please, that's a joke!"

A bumblebee fumbles with nectar-sipping trials,
While tulips wear shades and bask with wide smiles.
A rabbit in plaid shares his latest affairs,
About dreams of finding grand carrots in layers.

In a world bursting colors, with mishaps galore,
The whimsy keeps growing, a never-ending score.
With vignettes of laughter, we twirl through the day,
In a floral delight that just won't drift away!

A Journey on Gossamer Wings

With a hiccup and a giggle, we soar,
Chasing clouds that roll on the floor.
Butterflies play peek-a-boo in the breeze,
While we barter with squirrels for pecans and cheese.

In this flight of fancy, we trip over air,
Laughter ensnares us, without any care.
We'll sip on the sunshine, toast the odd moon,
And dance with the shadows of an afternoon.

Tickle the daisies, sing songs to the sky,
Let's paint our adventures, oh my, oh my!
With rainbows as surfboards on puddles we ride,
The laughter keeps lifting us higher with pride.

So bring out the giggles, the sparkle, the fun,
Every twist of the journey is never quite done.
On gossamer wings we'll forever remain,
In a world spun together with whimsy and rain.

The Lightness of Being

With jellybean sandals, I hop, oh so light,
Chasing my shadow through the day and the night.
Each flip of my hair sends the birds into flight,
A giggle escapes as I tickle the bright.

Clouds wear my wishes like hats in the sun,
A parade made of laughter, a whimsical run.
In the circus of life, I'm the headlining act,
Each tumble and stumble, a ticklish fact.

Butterflies swear they know the latest dance,
While I stumble and fumble in joyous romance.
A polka-dot picnic with cupcakes that sing,
All the whimsy that life can hilariously bring.

So wrap me in sunshine, in sprinkles and glee,
Let's frolic forever, just you, me, and tea.
With a bounce in our steps, we'll twirl and we'll swing,
Embracing the lightness of wonderfully funny things.

In the Heart of a Fragrant Day

Bumbles and giggles in the petal-filled park,
Where the sun shines as bright as the glittering lark.
We'll prance with our sandwiches, free-spirited friends,
Creating a ruckus that never quite ends.

The breeze carries echoes of laughter and cheer,
As bees act like comedians buzzing near.
We juggle our juices, slip-glide on grass,
Finding joy in the small things, like dolls made of glass.

A sunbeam of silliness spills on the ground,
As we chase after shadows, all silly and round.
Every whiff of the flowers elicits a grin,
In this fragrant adventure, pure joy can begin.

So let's make a memory, let's frolic, let's sway,
In the heart of this garden, let humor hold sway.
With each giggly moment, let's bloom and let play,
In this fragrant explosion, we'll dance the day away.

Impressions of Sunlit Whispers

Twirling in circles, our giggles take flight,
Cotton candy clouds hover, oh what a sight!
And whispers of sunshine tell secrets to bees,
While we sip on the laughter, sweet breezes and teas.

A ticklish tick-tock from the clocks in the trees,
Every hour a jester, with tricks and with tease.
We'll tumble through daisies, slip-slide on dew,
And share all our dreams over snacks made for two.

The wind weaves a story of laughter and cheer,
Petals dance like ballerinas, swirling near.
With a wink and a nudge, the universe jives,
In this whimsical realm, it's where fun truly thrives.

So come, let's dip toes in the puddles of light,
In impressions of laughter, everything feels right.
With sunlit whispers and echoes of fun,
Let's paint our adventures, till the day is done.

Dreamscapes Drenched in Color

A squirrel is wearing my hat,
He thinks he's fashionable, you see.
The flowers giggle, how absurd,
As butterflies sip herbal tea.

A rabbit hops, a dance unfolds,
He twirls in circles, what a sight!
The bees all buzz in harmony,
Creating tunes, a sweet delight.

A sunbeam slips through leafy green,
It tickles noses, what a tease!
I chase the light, my smile wide,
Tripping over bumblebees!

In this weird world, I find my glee,
Where colors blend with silly prance.
With every step, a laugh erupts,
A comic tale of chance and dance.

Musing Under a Canopy of Blooms

Beneath a tree, I lay in thought,
Looking up at petals bright.
A ladybug plays chess with me,
Her moves are bold, but not too tight.

A brazen crow starts to caw,
With flair, he struts like he's the king.
My sandwich stolen by the wind,
I laugh at nature's funny fling.

A snail slides by, slow as a song,
He's got the time, no hurry here.
I sip my tea, a butterfly
Lands on my nose, what a weird cheer!

Amongst the blooms, the laughter grows,
Life's humor wrapped in vibrant hues.
Musing here, I twirl with mirth,
In this daydream, I can't lose.

Footprints on a Canvas of Flora

I stepped in paint, oh what a mess,
My shoes are now a wild array.
Each print a splash of vivid fun,
A masterpiece for bees to play.

With every hop, they float around,
Like tiny jesters in a show.
They giggle loud, I laugh along,
My toes dipped deep in nature's glow.

A frog joins in, dressed like a chef,
He stirs the air with zestful croaks.
We paint the world with leaps and bounds,
Creating laughter from our jokes.

In fields of green, we dance like fools,
With flowers swaying to our tune.
My footprints trace a funny tale,
Beneath the sun, we'll make it noon.

The Art of Surrendering to Bliss

With arms wide open to the breeze,
I give in to this vibrant joy.
The world around begins to spin,
Like it's a never-ending toy.

A squirrel tosses acorns high,
As if they're confetti from above.
Each plop and drop is pure delight,
A woodland party full of love.

Dandelions float like wishes,
While giggles bloom from every side.
Nature paints my silly grin,
As I embrace the playful ride.

So here I am, in blissful sway,
Dancing wildly in the sun.
This canvas bright holds moments dear,
A joyful heart, a life of fun.

Secrets Beneath the Blushing Boughs

Beneath the trees so bright and pink,
The squirrels gather for coffee and drink.
They gossip and giggle, a fluffy parade,
While dreaming of acorns and tongues that trade.

A bee in a bowtie takes charming flight,
Inspects all the flowers, it's quite a sight.
He flirts with the petals, oh what a buzz,
But make him a honey, and hear all the fuzz.

The rabbits play cards, their tails in a flap,
Betting on carrots while taking a nap.
Their laughter erupts like a bubbling brook,
With cookies for bribes, old friendship's the hook.

Beneath the boughs, laughter dances free,
As critters concoct their own jubilee.
Secrets exchanged within nature's own mirth,
In this hidden world, they reign over earth.

A Tapestry of Dreamscapes

In a sky stitched with clouds and glee,
A llama in pajamas sips mango tea.
He croons to the stars that twinkle above,
Each note sends ripples of raucous love.

A fish on a bicycle pedals so spry,
Chasing a cat who is learning to fly.
They giggle together in wobbly tunes,
As jellybeans whirl like colorful balloons.

From sunlight spills tales of whimsical cheer,
While daisies wear hats and toast their own beer.
The breeze brings the laughter, a swirling delight,
In this velvety world, everything feels right.

With whimsical whimsy and mischief galore,
Each dream is a dance, who could ask for more?
In a tapestry woven with threads of pure fun,
The night winks at dreams beneath a bright sun.

The Silk of Sunset Whispers

In the glow of the evening, a frog takes a leap,
Reciting old rhymes that make daisies weep.
He wears a fine tux with a bright yellow tie,
While crickets provide a soft lullaby.

The fireflies waltz with a giggly little bat,
Who thinks he's a dancer, imagine that!
They twirl through the dusk with a flicker and flash,
A ballet of laughter, oh what a splash!

A hedgehog in leggings joins in the show,
His moves are ridiculous, we all say, whoa!
He tumbles and tumbles, rolls left and then right,
Declaring himself the king of the night.

So under the hues of a whimsical sky,
The laughter spreads wide, let's give it a try.
In whispers of silk that flutter and sing,
The magic of dusk makes the night feel like spring.

Dandelions and Other Fantasies

In fields where the wind sends wishes to roam,
A goat with a monocle makes himself home.
With dandelion dreams sprouting all around,
He juggles his thoughts while spinning profound.

A snail dressed in stripes plays tag with the sun,
While mice in tiny hats are radishing fun.
They race for a cookie, the marathon prize,
With laughter that echoes across endless skies.

The butterflies gossip, a fluttering choir,
Sharing the secrets of love and empire.
With wings painted bright, they dance like a breeze,
Leaving trails of humor that tickle the trees.

So gather your giggles, let joy take its flight,
With whimsy and wonder, the world feels so right.
In dandelion fields where magic won't cease,
Our hearts find a rhythm, a jubilant peace.

The Dance of Gentle Fragrance

In the air, a scent so sweet,
Slightly sticky like a treat.
Bumblebees dance with their flair,
Sipping nectar without a care.

A breeze twirls petals around,
Like confetti without a sound.
Squirrels pause mid-chatter, bop,
Wondering when the fun will stop.

Blossoms giggle in the sun,
Chasing shadows just for fun.
Even ants try to groove along,
Marching to their tiny song.

Underneath the joyous trees,
A turnip dreams of honeybees.
Flower crowns for all to share,
Nature's jesters everywhere.

Moments in Blossom's Embrace

Fluffy clouds drift by with glee,
Alicia tries to climb a tree.
Her hat flies off, the breeze is sly,
A nearby twirl makes her cry.

Petals whisper, 'What a show!'
As she stumbles, lights aglow.
Laughter echoes through the park,
While robins chirp a silly lark.

Chasing dreams on tiptoe feet,
Wishing starlight tasted sweet.
Cherry jam on toast, oh dear!
Sticky fingers, bursting cheer.

Sunlight peeks, a friendly pat,
As she models quite a hat.
Blossoms chuckle, squinting bright,
Creating joy from morning light.

Flurries of Pink and Bright Imagination

Around the yard, a frolic play,
Pink and fluff, a fun ballet.
Dancing squirrels, laugh so spry,
Catching dreams as they pass by.

A hedgehog spins, full of sass,
While rabbits hop and dance en masse.
Cotton candy skies above,
Make everyone feel the love.

Imagined worlds in bloom and air,
Twirling thoughts without a care.
Lemonade and jubilant shouts,
Compliments to occasional sprout.

Laughter spills like morning dew,
Whispers of fortunes made anew.
A charming dream, all cheers and glee,
As petals flutter, wild and free.

Fragments of Sunlit Wishes

Sunrays tickle the flowers' face,
Every insect joins the race.
A wishing well, a floppy hat,
Leaves rustle here, imagine that!

Dandelions puff like clouds,
Chasing giggles, drawing crowds.
Was that a hop or just a twirl?
Oops! That's grandma, give a whirl!

Frogs croak symphonies on logs,
Jolly taverns for the frogs.
Bubbles popping like the sun,
Sing along, let's have some fun!

With every swirl, a wish takes flight,
Laughter echoes, hearts feel light.
In every corner, joy persists,
Chasing sunsets, topping lists.

Whispers Beneath the Floral Canopy

Underneath a pink parade,
A bumblebee made quite a raid.
It buzzed around my sandwich slice,
Declaring lunch a game of dice.

The petals danced in gentle breeze,
While squirrels debated over cheese.
A butterfly stole my last fry,
I chuckled as it zipped on by.

Beneath the blooms, I lost my hat,
It flew away—imagine that!
With petals raining on my head,
I wondered if I'd soon be wed!

A ladybug with shades so cool,
Taught me the art of being a fool.
"Life's too short," it winked at me,
"To fuss too much with form and spree!"

A Reverie in Petal Hues

In colors bright, the world's a joke,
With giggles hiding in the oak.
A squirrel wore a tiny cap,
As if to say, "No time for nap!"

With blossoms swirling in the air,
I laughed as they tousled my hair.
A robin chirped a tune so spry,
It nearly made my heart fly high.

I spotted ants in tiny suits,
Performing merry little hoots.
"Let's dance!" I said, and joined the crew,
In this absurdity, beauty grew.

The sun peeked down with playful glee,
"Join me now in this jubilee!"
A flowered crown upon my head,
I twirled and thought, "I'm being fed!"

Tendrils of Soft Spring Light

Sunshine tickled the grass so green,
While I danced like a silly teen.
A butterfly, my partner true,
Pretended we were in the zoo.

An ant informed me of a plot,
To steal my snacks, oh what a thought!
With laughter, we set up a feast,
And called in critters, to say the least.

A froggy friend croaked out a beat,
While rabbits joined, tapping their feet.
We formed a band beneath the skies,
With nature's giggles as our prize.

The shadows danced as evening crept,
And into dreams we softly stepped.
"Tomorrow let's do it again!"
I grinned, knowing joy knows no end.

The Enchanted Orchard's Song

In the orchard where laughter plays,
Fruit hangs low on funny days.
A gopher juggled grapes with flair,
Not a care, just sweetened air!

The wind chimed in, a playful friend,
Whispering secrets that never end.
"Catch a breeze, join this merry game,
Life's a circus, not a shame!"

With giggles echoing everywhere,
The blossoms twirled like they didn't care.
I bowed to nature's wild delight,
Who knew daytime dreaming felt so right?

The sun bid adieu with a wink,
As we danced and swayed on the brink.
A final laugh, a burst of cheer,
In this enchanted place, it's clear!

Reflections on a Petal-Laden Breeze

A breeze so soft, it tickles your nose,
Whispers of laughter as the petals propose.
A dance with the wind, a giggly affair,
Nature's confetti flutters through the air.

Silly thoughts spin like the twirling leaves,
Do flowers gossip? Oh, what a tease!
Chasing the clouds, we tumble and play,
In a world where worries just drift away.

Under the sun, we wear childish grins,
Pretending to fly, where the fun never ends.
Every drop of dew, a glimmering joke,
In this garden of whimsy, spirits evoke.

With petals as pillows, we'll nap without care,
In this quirky haven, let's slumber and share.
For each little bud seems to wink and to say,
Let's laugh at the chaos that colors our day.

Where Time Finds Its Lull

Tick-tock goes the clock, but who really cares,
With the scent of sweet blooms trailing up the stairs?
Time takes a break, for fun is the call,
As we giggle and frolic, we'll ignore it all.

In the sun's warm embrace, we roll on the grass,
Counting the clouds as they drift and they pass.
A dragon-shaped fluff, then a turtle appears,
We'll giggle aloud, perhaps shed some tears.

Rainbows burst forth like a cheerful surprise,
The sky's a fine canvas, painted with sighs.
So let's grab some colors, and splash them about,
In this timeless escape, we'll laugh and we'll shout.

Someday grown-ups will pull us from play,
But today we'll just linger, come what may.
In this pocket of joy, where seconds don't dwell,
Let's twirl in our bliss, cast a fun-loving spell.

Garden of Fleeting Allure

In a garden so bright, with a smile like a sun,
Every flower is grinning, oh, aren't we having fun?
Bees buzz like comedians, flitting with glee,
As we share silly secrets, just you and me.

The daisies are giggling, the tulips, they tease,
With petals like umbrellas, floating in ease.
A hopscotch of laughter leaps from bloom to bloom,
In this whimsical paradise where joy finds its room.

Butterflies flutter, like dancers in flight,
Chasing each other beneath the soft light.
A chorus of colors all sing out aloud,
Inviting us close, in their whimsical crowd.

So let's toast to the daisies, the grass, and the sky,
With lemonade laughter and firefly sighs.
For in this fleeting wonder, we find our delight,
Let's dance 'til the stars sprinkle magic at night.

Lifting the Veil of Slumber

When morning steals in with a cheeky grin,
It tickles your toes, let the daydreams begin.
A sleepy-eyed giggle, the world is alive,
As petals like pillows help us to thrive.

We stretch like the daisies that yawningly bloom,
In this garden of chuckles, there's never a gloom.
The sun's a bright jester, all who wander around,
In the symphony of laughter, pure joy is found.

With a hop and a skip, we float through the morn,
Chasing wild butterflies that dance and adorn.
Each leaf is a whisper, each stem a soft cheer,
In this playful realm, we have nothing to fear.

So let's sip on the sunshine, and dance with the breeze,
Write silly poems beneath the tall trees.
For in this sweet moment, we'll let our hearts play,
And lift the soft veil that sleeps on the day.

The Harmony of Nature's Breath

In a garden where giggles grow,
Petals dance in a breezy show,
Bees wear tiny hats, oh so bright,
Buzzing tunes in pure delight.

Squirrels argue over sunshine,
While butterflies sip nectar, just divine,
A sunbeam tickles a sleepy cat,
As the flowers chat, 'Can you believe that?'

The breeze whispers jokes to the trees,
They chuckle along with the buzzing bees,
A dandelion's crown feels special today,
While the daisies giggle and sway.

Mirth blooms like flowers, wild and free,
In this patch of color, a sight to see,
All nature conspiring, a joyful quest,
Where laughter and joy can never rest.

A Spell of Floral Mischief

Twisting vines, with tricks up their sleeves,
Playing pranks on the soft autumn leaves,
A cheeky bud winks at a passing bee,
Throwing pollen like confetti with glee.

Crickets chirp in merry debate,
Who makes the best wriggle and shake?
While tulips gossip about the pink sky,
And birds laugh at the clouds drifting by.

A daisied fairy juggles with glee,
Her flowers droop, not caring to flee,
As she trips on a root and falls with a splash,
Sending petals flying in a riotous crash.

Nature's laughter rings loud and clear,
As blossoms conspire without any fear,
In this uproar, mischievous we find,
A vibrant spell of frolic designed.

Where Wishes Blossom

A flower wishes on a drifting cloud,
It wants a crown, oh so proud,
The breeze snickers, 'Not today, pal!'
While daisies dance, a floral gal.

Sun-kissed petals in bright array,
Tickle the air like a child at play,
A butterfly daydreams on a leaf,
While ants debate their tiny belief.

Bumbling bees plot a make-believe show,
Dreaming of rainbows, glitter, and glow,
A sunbeam stumbles over a rose,
Tickling its thorns, 'Ouch!' it goes.

Wishes unfurl like bright-colored sails,
As petals conspire and tickle their tales,
In this world of whimsy, no dullness seen,
Just laughter and magic, pure and keen.

Elixirs of Sun and Shade

Sunshine spills like laughter bright,
While shadows play hide and seek at night,
A gopher drinks from a daisy cup,
As whispers of breezes twirl it up.

Petals mix their colors with flair,
In a whimsical brew, beyond compare,
A cheeky tulip brews lemonade,
While sunflowers sunbathe, carefree parade.

Butterflies in rainbow flights,
Stirring elixirs in the light,
A sassy fern rolls its leafy eyes,
At bees sipping nectar with clever lies.

In this potion of sun and shade,
Giggles abound, no charade,
A sweet concoction of joy we've made,
Where life's greatest moments are never delayed.

www.ingramcontent.com/pod-product-compliance
Lightning Source LLC
Chambersburg PA
CBHW070311120526
44590CB00017B/2635